THE
NOVEMBER
BABY

THE
November
BABY

★

Noel Streatfeild

First published in 1959
This edition published in 2023 by Headline Home
an imprint of Headline Publishing Group

1

Cataloguing in Publication Data is available from the British Library

Hardback ISBN 978 1 0354 0859 7
eISBN 978 1 0354 0860 3

Typeset in 14.75/15pt Centaur MT Pro by Jouve (UK), Milton Keynes

Printed and bound in Great Britain by Clays Ltd, Elcograf S.p.A.

Headline's policy is to use papers that are natural, renewable and recyclable
products and made from wood grown in well-managed forests and other
controlled sources. The logging and manufacturing processes are expected
to conform to the environmental regulations of the country of origin.

HEADLINE PUBLISHING GROUP
An Hachette UK Company
Carmelite House
50 Victoria Embankment
London EC4Y 0DZ

www.headline.co.uk
www.hachette.co.uk

CONTENTS

THE November baby has arrived, telephones have been ringing, messages have flown to and fro like butterflies. All the usual questions have been asked. 'Is it a boy or a girl?' 'What does it weigh?' 'Has it any hair?' 'Who, if anybody, does it take after?' Now the moment has arrived when the news is circulated, 'There may be visitors,' and the question is what present shall I take?

Of course the right present is baby clothes, but how few of us hold on to the baby clothes we have bought or made until the actual arrival? The temptation to send them in advance is overwhelming.

Flowers are a perfect present, but let us face it, November is not a good month for them. There are of course carnations, roses, and such in the flower shops, but they are expensive, and with the chrysanthemums nearly over, and the forced spring flowers not yet arrived, it is difficult to buy a

satisfactory vase full that is within the reach of the leaner purse.

The same goes for fruit. There may be exotics to be bought, but the season is with us again of oranges, apples, bananas, and grapes, which however tastefully arranged still look like oranges, apples, bananas, and grapes, and it is easy to get tired of them. Also a plethora of these fruits can be a glut in the hospital or nursing home: summer fruits can so easily be

given away, but the winter regulars are harder to place.

That leaves books, which must in the old leisured days of a month in bed have been the perfect present. But nowadays what with the time in bed being cut by at least half, and exercises and massage added to the daily round, mothers complain they have no time to read, that what is needed is something more in the way of a snack than a whole book.

It was years of wondering 'What present shall I take her?', together with the request for short reading, which has produced this book. What most mothers talk about, and therefore presumably like to read about, is Baby. Here

then, as an offering for you, is all the information I could collect about babies of yesterday and today who were born in November. The book starts with a list of names. 'Goodness,' you may say, 'I don't need any help with names, we chose the names for either a boy or a girl months ago.' You may

have, but plenty of parents are still undecided after the baby has arrived. Some have determined on a girl, when what has turned up is a boy, and vice versa, so the wrong names are ready. Some have a name in view, but it does not go with the surname, and needs another name added. Some just haven't a clue. Anyway, for all who need help, here is a long list of names, all in some way connected with November.

Few of us can resist studying the stars under which we were born, and it is natural to look at those belonging to the new baby. But to unsettle those who believe in the stars, and to amuse those who do not, the information about those born under Scorpio and those born under Sagittarius is followed by a list of some of the distinguished people born on each day in the month, and very surprising reading much of it is. Would you expect an artist whose vision was so widely different as that of Hogarth, to share a birthday with Epstein? And though they are all Scorpio babies, no one is going to convince me Lady Caroline Lamb had much in common with Stevenson, or that Petula Clark and Rommel would jump to the mind as born under the same stars. But for those who believe in the stars, the 30th is worth studying. Who could be more fitted to share a birthday than Sir Philip Sidney and Sir Winston Churchill? Now turn to your baby's birthday and see if you approve of those who share it.

NAMES
for the
NOVEMBER
BABY

NOVEMBER was the ninth month in the Roman year. The girl's name *Nona* means 'ninth'.

The Saxons had another name for November: they called it 'wind-month', *Keith* means 'wind'. November is too a dark and grey month, so how about *Nigel* which means 'dark', or *Lloyd* which means 'grey'?

One of the signs of the zodiac for November is Sagittarius. Sagittarius was of course a mythical archer, so how about *Archer* for a boy? People born under this sign are supposed to excel at sport, so here are some names which mean 'champion'. *Neal, Neil* or *Neill,* and *Nelson* mean 'son of a champion'. *Thurlow* means 'Thor's sport'. Roman victors were crowned with laurel leaves: *Lawrence* and *Laurence* mean 'laurel', and so do the girls' names *Laura, Lauren* and *Lauretta. Olympia* and *Olympus* come from Mount Olympus, which suggests the Olympic Games. *Ernest* means 'vigour', *Brian, Brien* and *Bryan* mean 'strength', *Connor* and *Conor* 'great strength', and *Kean* 'vast'.

Matthias is the special apostle for November. *Matthias,* or the more usual name *Matthew,* mean 'gift of Jehovah'.

The 1st of November is All Saints' Day, so the name of any saint fits a November baby. If the baby is English one of England's patron saints would be a good choice. They are St George, Protector of the Kingdom, Peter the Apostle, and Edward the Confessor. The name *George* means 'tiller of the soil'. *Geordie* is a variant, and *Yorick* means the same. For girls the name becomes *Georgia, Georgiana* and *Georgina. Peter* means 'stone'. Other names with similar meanings are *Miles* which means 'millstone', *Stanley*

'stony meadow', and *Wystan* 'battle-stone'. *Edward* means 'rich ward'. Just plain *Ward* is a possible boy's name. If the baby is Welsh, the patron saint is of course St David. *David* means 'friend', *Alwyn* and *Aylwin* mean 'noble friend', *Carmichael* 'friend of Michael', and *Bonamy* 'good friend'. *Edwin* and *Edwina* mean 'rich friend', *Cara* 'friend', and *Elvina* 'friendly'. *Godwin* means 'God-friend', and *Mervin* or *Mervyn* 'famous friend'.

If the baby is Irish St Patrick is the saint to name him after. *Patrick* or Patric, and *Patricia* mean 'patrician', and so does *Padraic.*

Australia and New Zealand have three patron saints, Our Lady Help of Christians, Francis Xavier, and Patrick. *Mary* means 'wished-for child', and has many variations: *Maria, Marian, Mariann, Marie, Mariel, Marion, Marlene, Marylyn, Maura, Maureen* and *Maurine. Francis* means 'free', and so do *Frances, Francesca* and *Frank.*

The patron saints of Canada are St Ann and St George. *Ann* means 'God has favoured me', and so do *Anne, Anita, Anna, Annette* and *Annie.*

St Thomas the Apostle is said to have brought Christianity to India. *Thomas* means 'twin'.

The patron saint of children is St Nicholas of Myra. *Nicholas* means 'victory of the people', as do *Nicol, Nicola, Nicolette* and *Colette.*

Boys have one patron saint of their own, Aloysius Gonzaga. *Aloysius* means 'famous war'. Girls have two saints assigned to them, St Agnes and St Ursula. *Agnes* means 'pure'; *Annot* is another form of it. *Ursula* means 'little bear'.

Everyone knows that the 5th of November celebrates the discovery of the Gunpowder

Plot, so *Guy* is a likely name for a baby boy born on this day: it means 'leader'.

The 6th of November is St Leonard's Day. *Leonard* means 'strong as a lion', and here are other names with similar meanings: *Leander* which means 'lion-man', *Leo* and *Leon* 'lion', *Lionel* 'little lion', and *Llewellyn* or *Llewelyn* 'lion-like'.

The 11th of November is St Martin's Day or Martinmas. *Martin* comes from the Roman god of war Mars, and so do *Marcel, Marcellus, Marcus, Marc, Marius, Marcella, Marcia, Martina* and *Martine*. Martinmas was once commonly a time for hiring farm and other servants. *Lance* and *Lancelot* mean 'boy-servant', and *Rodney* 'road-servant'.

St Hugh's Day is the 17th of November.

Hugh means 'mind', and so does *Hugo*. *Hubert* means 'of bright mind'.

The 20th of November is Edmund's Day; he was both king and saint. *Edmund* or *Edmond* mean 'rich protection', and *Eamon* is the Irish form of it. *Egmond* and *Egmont* mean 'sword-protection', *Esmond* and *Osmond* 'divine protection', and *Ray* or *Raymond* 'wise protection'.

St Cecilia's Day is the 22nd of November. Cecilia is the patroness of both music and poetry. Other forms of *Cecilia* are *Cecilie, Cecily, Sisley,* or *Cecil* for a boy. It has been suggested that *Celia* and *Celine* are derived from *Cecilia,* but they may also have the meaning 'the heavens'.

The 23rd of November is St Clement's Day. *Clement* means 'merciful', and so do *Clemence* and *Clementine.*

St Catherine's Day is the 25th of November. *Catherine* means 'pure', and so do *Catharine, Cathleen, Catlin, Karen, Kate, Katharine, Katherine, Kathleen, Katrine* and *Kay.*

The 30th of November is St Andrew's Day. *Andrew* means 'man', and unexpectedly *Charles* has the same meaning, and so have *Carol,*

Carlo and *Carla*. *Adam* means 'a man' (and *Eve* 'lively'). *Carola, Carolina, Caroline* and *Carolyn* are the feminine forms of *Charles,* and have come to mean 'woman'.

The birthstone for November is the topaz. What an original name *Topaz* would make for a baby girl, or how about *Amber*?

GIFTS
for the
NOVEMBER
BABY

IF a godparent or other well-wisher would like to give the baby a piece of jewellery, the right gift for the November baby is the topaz, which is the emblem of fidelity. Mothers of November babies will probably be very envious that their child has chosen such a varied birthstone, for though the topaz runs through all the colours of sunshine and sherry, there are other kinds to be had in pink, red, green, blue and brown, so whatever your baby's favourite colour turns out to be later on, there is a topaz to match it. Leonardus found several other uses for the stone, and here is what he wrote in 1750 about it in *The Mirror of Stones*:

'If the Topaz is thrown into Water boiling hot, it quickly cools, and that by this Coolness lascivious Motions are quell'd. It's a Cure for the Phrensy, cleanses the Hemorrhoids, cures and prevents Lunacy, increases Riches, assuages Anger and Sorrow, and averts Sudden Death . . . it makes the Bearer of it obtain the Favour of Princes.'

The old custom of sending flowers so that they bring a message should be revived for a November baby. For if your child should receive a bunch of laurel the meaning is Glory.

If your baby was born between the 1st and the 22nd of November read pages 24 and 25, but if between the 23rd and the 30th skip to pages 26 and 27.

UNDER
WHAT STARS WAS
MY BABY
BORN?

SCORPIO
The Scorpion

24th October–22nd November

SAGITTARIUS
The Archer

23rd November–21st December

CAPRICORN
The Sea Goat

22nd December–20th January

AQUARIUS
The Water Bearer

21st January–19th February

PISCES
The Fishes

20th February–20th March

ARIES
The Ram

21st March–20th April

TAURUS
The Bull

21st April–21st May

GEMINI
The Twins

22nd May–21st June

CANCER
The Crab

22nd June–23rd July

LEO
The Lion

24th July–23rd August

VIRGO
The Virgin

24th August–23rd September

LIBRA
The Scales

24th September–23rd October

Scorpio — the Scorpion
24th October–22nd November

PEOPLE born under Scorpio have strong and well-defined personalities. Passionate and wilful, they are at the same time reserved to the point of secretiveness. In them love easily turns to jealousy and anger to resentment. Their feelings are keen rather than tender. Dignity in appearance and in behaviour expresses their great self-esteem. They select as friends only those to whom they can extend some of this esteem, so their friendships are few but correspondingly firm. In thinking they are detailed and persistent, and if their instinct for the physical organism inclines them to medicine as a profession, one would expect them to be outstanding in it.

For the Scorpio Baby

Lucky to wear garnet, bloodstone.
Lucky stone is flint.
Lucky metal is iron.
The Scorpio baby's colour is red.
Lucky number is 9.
Luckiest day is Tuesday.

Sagittarius — the Archer
23rd November–21st December

PEOPLE born under Sagittarius are active, both physically and mentally. They are most at home out of doors, have a preference for work in the open air and are keen on sports. They are kind-hearted, sympathetic and impulsive, somewhat indiscriminate in their choice of friends. They do demand sincerity in others though, and are quick to note the lack of it. This acute power of insight is indeed so developed in some

Sagittarius people as to amount almost to a gift of prophecy. Physically Sagittarians are well-formed. Their facial expression is open and pleasing, their eyes always remarkable. They talk freely and love light-heartedly.

For the Sagittarius Baby

Lucky to wear chrysolite, uncut and deep amethyst, carbuncle.
Lucky stones are granite, sandstone.
Lucky metal is tin.
The Sagittarius baby's colour is violet.
Lucky number is 3.
Luckiest day is Thursday.

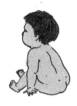

BABIES BORN
ON
THE SAME DAY
AS
YOUR BABY

SHOULD you feel pleased that your baby was born on a particular day? Is there any truth in what the astrologers say about some birthdays having special advantages, that babies born under Scorpio are like this, whereas babies born under Sagittarius are like that? Have a look at the well-known people in this list before you decide.

1st   Edward V, 1470. Benvenuto Cellini, 1500. John Strype, 1643. Mary Brunton, 1778. Madame Albani, 1852. Lord Balfour of Inchrye, 1897.

2nd   Marie Antoinette, 1755. Edward, Duke of Kent, 1767. Burt Lancaster, 1913.

3rd   Daniel Rutherford, 1749. Leopold III of Belgium, 1901. André Malraux, 1901. Jennie Lee, 1904.

4th	Mary Princess of Orange, 1631. William of Orange, 1650. Edmund Kean, 1787. Carlo Blasis, 1803. Sir Frank Benson, 1858. Eden Phillpotts, 1862.
5th	Hans Sachs, 1494. Vivien Leigh, 1913.
6th	Julian, Roman Emperor, 331. Colley Cibber, 1671. Ignace Jan Paderewski, 1860. Viscount Samuel, 1870. Raymond Postgate, 1896.
7th	Madame Curie, 1867. Albert Camus, 1913. Wolf Mankowitz, 1924.
8th	Edmund Halley, 1656. Elizabeth Christine, Queen of Prussia, 1715. Edward Robert Bulwer-Lytton, Earl of Lytton, 1831.
9th	Isabella of France, 2nd Queen of Richard II, 1389. William Sotheby, 1757. Ivan Turgenev, 1818. Emile Gaboriau, 1835. Edward VII, 1841. Sir Giles Gilbert Scott, 1880.
10th	Mahomet, 570. Martin Luther, 1483. Robert Devereux, Earl of Essex, 1566. William Hogarth, 1697. Oliver Goldsmith, 1728. Friedrich von Schiller, 1759. Vachel Lindsay, 1879. Jacob Epstein, 1880. Richard Burton, 1925.

11th   Georgiana, Lady Chatterton, 1806. Alfred de Musset, 1810. Fyodor Dostoievski, 1821. Gustav VI Adolph, King of Sweden, 1882. René Clair, 1898.

12th   Saint Augustine, 313. Amelia Opie, 1769. Aleksandr Borodin, 1834. Maureen Gardner, 1928. Princess Grace of Monaco, 1929.

13th   Edward III, 1312. Philip 'the Magnanimous', Landgrave of Hesse, 1504. Lady Caroline Lamb, 1785. Edward John Trelawny, 1792. James Clerk Maxwell, 1831. Robert Louis Stevenson, 1850. Major-General Iskander Mirza, 1899. Hermione Baddeley, 1906.

14th   Omobono Stradivari, 1679. Claude Monet, 1840. Pandit Jawaharlal Nehru, 1889. Sir Frederick Grant Banting, 1891. Arthur Michael Ramsey, Archbishop of York, 1904. Prince Charles, 1948.

15th   Petula Clark, 1932. William Pitt, Lord Chatham, 1708. Sir William Herschel, 1738. Rommel, 1891. Aneurin Bevan, 1897.

16th   Tiberius, Roman Emperor, 42 B.C. Jean le Rond d'Alembert, 1707. John Bright, 1811. Paul Hindemith, 1895. Sir Oswald Mosley, 1896.

17th   Vespasian, Roman Emperor, 9 A.D. Field-Marshal Viscount Montgomery, 1887.

18th   W. S. Gilbert, 1836. Cezare Lombroso, 1836. Frank Dobson, 1888. Alan T. Lennox-Boyd, 1904.

19th   Charles I, 1600. Ferdinand de Lesseps, 1805. Phyllis Bentley, 1894. Anton Walbrook, 1896.

20th   Thomas Chatterton, 1752. Margaret of Savoy, queen of Humbert I of Italy, 1851. Alistair Cooke, 1908. Bobby Locke, 1917.

21st   Voltaire, 1694. Sir Samuel Cunard, 1787. Sir Arthur Quiller-Couch, 1863.

22nd   Richard Neville, Earl of Warwick, 1428. Mary of Guise, queen of James V of Scotland, 1515. Isabella, queen of Philip IV of Spain, 1602. Mrs Dora Jordan, 1761. George Eliot, 1819. André Gide, 1869. General Charles de Gaulle,

1890. Benjamin Britten, 1913. Anne Crawford, 1920. Pat Smythe, 1928.

23rd Thomas Lord, 1755. François Noël Babeuf, 1760. The Marquess of Carisbrooke, 1886. Boris Karloff, 1887. Harpo Marx, 1888.

24th Baruch Spinoza, 1632. Laurence Sterne, 1713. Grace Darling, 1815. Frances Hodgson Burnett, 1849. Toulouse-Lautrec, 1864.

25th Lope de Vega, 1562. Queen Henrietta Maria, 1609. Catherine of Braganza, 1638. Andrew Carnegie, 1835. Anastas Ivanovich Mikoyan, 1895.

26th William Cowper, 1731. Emlyn Williams, 1905.

27th Madame de Maintenon, 1635. Mary Robinson ('Perdita'), 1758. Fanny Kemble, 1809. Sir William Orpen, 1878.

28th William Blake, 1757. Countess Mountbatten of Burma, 1901. Keith R. Miller, 1919.

29th Margaret Tudor, queen of James IV of Scotland, 1489. Jean Baptiste Lully, circa 1633. Louisa M. Alcott, 1832. Jean Martin Charcot, 1825.

30th   Sir Philip Sidney, 1554. Jonathan Swift, 1667. Theodor Mommsen, 1817. Mark Twain, 1835. Sir Winston Churchill, 1874. Lord Adrian, 1889. Geoffrey Household, 1900.

THE UPBRINGING OF NOVEMBER BABIES OF THE PAST

A VERY safe and pleasant change of diet is made for infants by the use of old-fashioned pap. It is an excellent help in giving beef-tea. But the pap must be properly made; it must not be merely soaked bread. For the use of those who are not experienced in nursery cooking, it may be an advantage to give the following rules for making it: –

A thick slice of bread must be crumbed into a basin, the basin filled with boiling water, a plate put on the top thereof, and the whole allowed to stand for twenty minutes. Then the water must be strained or poured off, and the bread put into a saucepan, with fresh cold water. This must boil for three and a half hours, during which time the cook must change the water three times, beating up the bread with a fork very often, and skimming off all the white liquid which boils on the surface. Then it may be strained through a fine sieve into a clean basin and set to cool. When cold, it will be a nice jelly. Pap should never be given with a spoon to a child under six months old. Sucked through the bottle, it is easy of digestion and very nourishing, but there are few infants able to digest it unless given in this manner.

Infant Life, by E. N. G., 1869.

CURE FOR THE HOOPING-COUGH. —'I know,' said one of my parishioners, 'what would cure him, but m'appen you woudent believe me.' 'What is it, Mary?' I asked. 'Why, I did every thing that every body teld me. One teld me to get him breathed on by a pie-bald

horse. I took him ever such a way, to a horse at ——, and put him under the horse's mouth; but he was no better. Then I was teld to drag him backward through a bramble bush. I did so; but this didn't cure him. Last of all, I was teld to give him nine fried mice, fasting, in a morning, in this way: — three the first morning; then wait three mornings, and then give him three more; wait three mornings, and then give him three more. When he had eaten these nine fried mice he became quite well. This would be sure to cure your child, Sir.'

A Correspondent, in
Notes & Queries, 1850.

ANOTHER REMEDY TO CURE A COUGH

Roast an onion, rub the soles of the feet therewith, and the ailment will cease; or take strong brandy, dip a soft cloth therein and wet the soles of the feet, morning and evenings.

Albertus Magnus, *White and Black
Art for Man and Beast*, 13th Century.

GUY FAWKES DAY

A writer in the Every Day Book, in 1826, says, 'scuffles seldom happen now, but in my youthful day, when guy met guy – then came the tug of war!' The partisans fought, and a decided victory ended in the capture of the guy belonging to the vanquished. Sometimes desperate bands, who omitted, or were destitute of the means to make 'guys,' went forth like

Froissart's knights upon adventures. An enterprise of this sort was called 'going to swing a guy', that is, to steal one by force of arms, by fists, and sticks, from its rightful owners. These partisans were always successful, for they always attacked the weak.

Pictorial Calendar of the Seasons, 1854.

One hardly meets with a girl who can at the same time boast of early performances with the needle, and a good constitution. Close and early confinement generally occasions indigestion, headaches, pale complexions, pain of the stomach, loss of appetite, coughs, consumptions of the lungs, and deformity of body. The last of these, indeed, is not to be wondered at, considering the awkward postures in which girls sit at many kinds of needlework, and the delicate flexible state of their bodies in the early periods of life.

. . . Would mothers, instead of having their daughters instructed in many trifling accomplishments, employ them in plain work and housewifery, and allow them sufficient exercise in the open air, they would both make them more healthy mothers, and more useful members of society. Accomplishments are very desirable, but they should be considered as secondary, and always disregarded when they impair health.

A Hand-Book of Domestic Medicine,
by an eminent physician, 1855.

To cure children of the measles, they must be passed three times over the back and under the belly of a bear. I had a servant whose mother thus treated him as a child. He was passed three times over the back and under the belly of a dancing bear which was being led about the roads.

Jackson, *Shropshire Folk-Lore,* 1883.

When the child begins to use a spoon, or to handle any object, let care be taken to make it use the right hand chiefly, and also accustom it to shake hands only by that hand. By these means it will soon learn that the right is the proper hand to employ, and in this respect will grow up faultless.

Barwell, *Infant Treatment,* 1840.

When a child is in a fit, put it into a hot bath, taking care that the water is not scalding, try it carefully first with the hand. Give an emetic of ipecacuanha, and afterwards two grains of calomel, then castor oil, or rhubarb and magnesia, so as completely to empty the stomach.

Kingston, *Infant Amusements,* 1867.

Before I leave this subject, I solemnly call upon all mothers, who are wont to transfer the formation of their daughters' minds to the hands of strangers, seriously to reflect upon what they are about. You have brought your child into the world, and you are answerable for the early impressions its infant mind shall receive. Is it too much to ask of you to make for your *own* peace, as well as that of your children, by giving an active attention in due time, when the mind is malleable, to the formation of your child's character, moral and intellectual, – an account of which will most surely be required at your hands! Remember, your daughters may play well, sing well, dance well, — may talk well, about German, or the opera, or this and that person, — finally, may flirt well, and catch husbands and get establishments, but, if they cannot *think well*, and act well, as Christian ladies ought to think and act, verily, after all, they are but as sounding brass or tinkling cymbals, sporting along the broad highway which leadeth to destruction!

The Mother the Best Governess,
London, 1839.

A ROYAL and A
DISTINGUISHED
NOVEMBER
BABY

EDWARD V
born November 1470.

IN the Wardrobe accounts for 1483, the year of the boy's accession to the throne, and murder in The Tower, is an entry to the following effect: –

'LORD EDWARD, SON TO THE LATE KING EDWARD IV, FOR HIS APPAREL AND ARRAY.

A short gown of crimson cloth of gold lined with black velvet, a long gown of crimson cloth of gold lined with green damask, a doublet and stomacher of black satin, a bonnet of purple velvet, nine horse harnesses and nine saddle housings of blue velvet, and magnificent apparel for his henchmen and pages.'

Strickland,
Lives of the Bachelor Kings, 1861.

GEORGIANA, LADY CHATTERTON
born November 1806.

I remember that one governess considered me unteachable, because I could not say the second Psalm by heart, and especially the verse, 'Why do the heathen so furiously rage?'

which she used to repeat over and over again to me in the vain endeavour to beat it into my head. The fact is, I was wondering all the time why the heathen did so furiously rage, and who they could be; so that the more my mind was made to dwell on the words, the more puzzled I became, and the less I remembered my lesson.

From her diary as quoted in *Memoirs of Georgiana, Lady Chatterton,* by Edward Heneage Dering, 1878.

DISTINGUISHED
NOVEMBER
BABIES

BENVENUTO CELLINI
born November 1500.

WHEN I was about five years of age, my father happened to be in a little room in which they had been washing, and where there was a good oak fire burning: with a fiddle in his hand he sang and played near the fire, the weather being exceedingly cold: he looked at this time into the flames, and saw a little animal resembling a lizard, which could live in the hottest part of that element: instantly perceiving what it was, he called for my sister, and after he had shewn us the creature, he gave me a box on the ear; I fell a crying, while he, soothing me with his caresses, spoke these words, 'My dear child, I don't give you that box for any fault you have committed, but that you may recollect that the little creature which you see in the fire is a Salamander; such a one as never was beheld before to my knowledge;' so saying he embraced me, and gave me some money.

The Autobiography of Benvenuto Cellini,
translation by T. Roscoe, 1822.

WILLIAM BLAKE
born November 1757.

On Peckham Rye (by Dulwich Hill) it is, as he will in after years relate, that while quite a

child, of eight or ten perhaps, he has his 'first vision'. Sauntering along, the boy looks up and sees a tree filled with angels, bright angelic wings bespangling every bough like stars. Returned home he relates the incident, and only through his mother's intercession escapes a thrashing from his honest father, for telling a lie.

Gilchrist, *Life of William Blake*, 1863.

LOUISA M. ALCOTT
born November 1832.

Needle-work began early, and at ten my skilful sister made a linen shirt beautifully;

while at twelve I set up as a doll's dressmaker, with my sign out and wonderful models in my window. All the children employed me, and my turbans were the rage at one time, to the great dismay of the neighbors' hens, who were hotly hunted down, that I might tweak out their downiest feathers to adorn the dolls' headgear.

Louisa M. Alcott: Her Life, Letters and Journals,
edited by Ednah D. Cheney, 1889.

WILLIAM COWPER
born November 1731.

At six years old I was taken from the nursery, and from the immediate care of a most indulgent mother, and sent to a considerable school in Bedfordshire. Here I had hardships of different kinds to conflict with, which I felt more sensibly, in proportion to the tenderness with which I had been treated at home. But my chief affliction consisted in my being singled out from all the other boys, by a lad about fifteen years of age, as a proper object upon whom he might let loose the cruelty of his temper. I choose to forbear a particular recital of the many acts of barbarity,

with which he made it his business continually
to persecute me: it will be sufficient to say,
that he had, by his savage treatment of me,
impressed such a dread of his figure upon
my mind, that I well remember being afraid
to lift up my eyes upon him, higher than his
knees; and that I knew him by his shoe-
buckles, better than any other part of his
dress. May the Lord pardon him, and may
we meet in glory!

Memoir of the Early Life of William Cowper.

THOMAS CHATTERTON
born November 1752.

Extract from a poem written by him at the
age of sixteen:

'I must confess, rejoins the prudent
    sage,
You're really something clever for your age;
Your lines have sentiment; and now and
    then
A dash of satire stumbles from your pen.
But ah! that satire is a dangerous thing,
And often wounds the writer with its
    sting;

Your infant muse should sport with other
   toys,
Men will not bear the ridicule of boys.'
       Chatterton: A Biographical Study, 1869.

SIR PHILIP SIDNEY
born November 1554.

From a letter he received from his father
in 1566:

'Be humble and obedient to yowr master, for
unless yow frame yowr selfe to obey others,
yea, and feale in yowr selfe what obedience
is, yow shall never be able to teach others how
to obey yow. Be curteese of gesture, and affable
to all men, with diversitee of reverence,
accordinge to the dignitie of the person. There
ys nothing, that wynneth so much with so
lytell cost. Use moderate dyet, so as, after yowr
meate, yow may find yowr wytte fresher and
not duller, and yowr body more lyvely, and not
more heavye. Seldom drinke wine, and yet
sometimes doe, least, being enforced to drinke
upon the sodayne, yow should find yowr self
inflamed. Use exercise of bodye, but such as ys
without peryll of yowr yointes or bones. It will

encrease your force, and enlardge yowr breathe. Delight to be cleanly, as well in all parts of yowr bodye, as in yowr garments. It shall make yow grateful in yche company, and otherwise lothsome. Give yowr self to be merye, for yow degenerate from yowr father, yf yow find not yowr self most able in wytte and bodye, to doe any thinge when yow be most mery: But let yowr myrthe be ever void of all scurilitee, and bitinge woords to any man, for an wound given by a woorde is oftentimes harder to be cured, then that which is given with the swerd.'

LUCY AIKIN
born November 1781.

One memorable day, my brother George, several years older, seized and devoured half of a tart destined for the supper of us two little ones. Fired at the injury, I ran with the fragment into the presence of papa and mamma, and denounced the offender in most emphatic terms. 'You should be willing to give your brother part of your tart,' said my mother. 'But he did not ask us,' I replied – 'he took it;' and I still think that the distinction was just, and that his action ought to have brought him, and not me, the reprimand. But how many fold was I compensated when my father, who had listened with great attention to my harangue, exclaimed, 'Why Lucy, you are quite eloquent!' O! never-to-be-forgotten praise! Had I been a boy, it might have made me an orator; as it was, it incited me to exert to the utmost, by tongue and by pen, all the power of words I possessed or could ever acquire – I had learned where my strength lay.

*Memoirs, Miscellanies and Letters of the
Late Lucy Aikin*,
edited by Le Breton, 1864.

FANNY KEMBLE
born November 1809.

And so to Boulogne I went, to a school in the oddly named 'Rue tant perd tant paie', in the old town, kept by a rather sallow and grim, but still vivacious old Madame Faudier, with the assistance of her daughter, Mademoiselle Flore, a bouncing, blooming beauty of a discreet age, whose florid complexion, prominent black eyes, plaited and profusely pomatumed black hair, and full, commanding figure, attired for fête days in salmon-coloured merino, have remained vividly impressed upon my memory. What I learned here, except French (which I could not help learning), I know not. I was taught music, dancing, and Italian, the latter by a Signor Mazzochetti, an object of special detestation to me, whose union with Mademoiselle Flore caused a temporary fit of rejoicing in the school. The small seven-year-old beginnings of such particular humanities I mastered with tolerable success, but if I may judge from the frequency of my *penitences,* humanity in general was not instilled into me without considerable trouble. I was a sore torment, no doubt, to poor Madame Faudier, who, on being once informed by some alarmed passers in the street that one of her 'demoiselles' was perambulating the house roof, is reported to have exclaimed, in a paroxysm of rage and terror, 'Ah, ce ne peut être que cette *diable* de Kemble!' and sure enough it was I. Having committed I know not what crime, I had been thrust for chastisement into a lonely garret, where, having nothing earthly to do but look about me, I discovered (like a prince in the Arabian Nights) a ladder leading to a trap-door, and presently was out on a sort of stone coping, which ran round the steep roof of the high, old-fashioned house, surveying with serene satisfaction the extensive prospect landward and seaward, unconscious that I was at the same time an object of terror to the beholders in the street below. Snatched from the perilous delight of this bad eminence, I was (again, I think, rather like the Arabian prince) forthwith plunged into the cellar; where I curled myself up on the upper step, close to the heavy door that had been locked upon me, partly for the comfort of the crack of light that squeezed itself through it, and partly, I suppose, from some vague idea that there was no bottom to the steps, derived from my own terror rather than from any precise historical knowledge of oubliettes and donjons, with the execrable treachery of stairs suddenly ending in mid-darkness over an abyss. I suppose I suffered a martyrdom of fear, for I remember upwards of thirty years afterwards having this very cellar, and my misery in it, brought before my mind suddenly, with intense vividness, while reading, in Victor Hugo's *Notre Dame*, poor Esmeralda's piteous entreaties for deliverance from her underground prison.

Frances Ann Kemble,
Record of a Girlhood, 1878.

EDMUND KEAN
born November 1787.

At not quite eight years of age . . . In the dead of night, with a few necessaries tied up in a bundle and slung over his shoulder on a stout stick, he left the house in Ewer-street, passed out of London, and made direct for the coast. As the sun rose he might have been seen trudging manfully along the road; and arrived at Portsmouth, he shipped himself as cabin boy on board a ship bound to Madeira.

The vessel had barely gone beyond sight of his native shores when the little sailor discovered that he had widely miscalculated the amount of labour to which he should be subjected in his new capacity. His tender years naturally rendered him unequal to the rigorous duties he had undertaken to discharge, and, disgusted and impatient with the servitude upon which he had voluntarily entered, he determined to effect his escape. The charm of 'Robinson Crusoe' was destroyed, and for a time his seafaring predilections were cured. The uncertainty of his return to England alone deterred him from abandoning the ship as it stopped at different ports on the way, and in the strategic means he ultimately adopted to emancipate himself from his unpleasant situation he showed that secretiveness was with him an inborn faculty. He represented that a cold contracted on board had produced a total deafness, and so well was the deception supported by every look and gesture, that captain and crew were alike deceived; but fearing that this infirmity might be deemed insufficient to preclude the performance of his duties, he further pretended that the aforesaid cold had settled in his extremities, producing a lameness that rendered him unable to leave his berth. The success of the last *ruse* was as unequivocal as its predecessor; he was permitted to keep his bed, and his wants were administered to. On the arrival of the ship at Madeira, he was removed to the hospital in that town, where, determined to maintain his assumed character to the last, he practised the deception for two months with so much care that all investigations into the nature of the malady were pronounced to be at fault. Cure was finally pronounced impossible, but as a kind of forlorn hope, the doctors, unconsciously playing into the hands of the interesting patient, prescribed his return to England. He was accordingly removed on board a homeward bound ship, and so firmly maintained his deceptive exterior throughout the voyage that not even the horrors of a tempest, which threatened every moment to engulph the ship in the surging waters, could induce him to turn otherwise than a *deaf* ear to the surrounding roar, or, in the endeavour to avert the destruction of the vessel, to participate in the bustle which prevails on a ship's deck during a storm.

Arrived on shore, he tendered his gratitude to those who had carried him from the ship by a sudden and vigorous execution of the college hornpipe, and disappeared amongst the ramifications of Portsmouth before his custodians recovered from the stupefying amazement into which they had been thrown by this unexpected evolution.

Hawkins, *The Life of Edmund Kean*, 1869.

GAMES
for the
NOVEMBER
BABY

KNEE-SONG

HERE goes my lord,
    A trot! A trot! a trot! a
        trot!
Here goes my lady,
A canter! a canter! a canter! a canter!
    Here goes my young master,
Jockey-hitch! jockey-hitch! jockey-hitch!
    jockey-hitch!
    Here goes my young miss,
An amble! an amble! an amble! an amble!
    The footman lags behind to tipple ale
        and wine,

And goes gallop, a gallop, a gallop, to
make up his time.

Popular Rhymes and Nursery Tales,
collected by Halliwell, 1849.

EVEN OR ODD?

This game is the most ancient, I think, that
we know. The children who played in the
streets of Athens and in the Roman Forum in
early ages knew and loved it, and little English
children find amusement in it still. It is played
in this manner: One child hides in her hand a
few beans, nuts, almonds, or even bits of
paper, and asks her companion to guess if
they are *odd* or *even.*

If the playfellow guesses *odd,* and on opening
her hand the other displays an *odd* number, she
forfeits the articles to the guesser, who hides
them in her turn; but if the guess is *odd,* and the
number *even,* the guesser pays a forfeit, and
the first hider retains the beans, &c. The guess
must be right to win.

Home Book of Pleasure and Instruction,
Jewry, 1867.

The teacher says 'a dead calm', all sit quite still and silent, with their fingers on their mouths; 'a breeze', all gently rub their hands together; 'a gale of wind', they go on rubbing their hands, and make at the same time a gentle hissing noise with their lips; 'a storm', they go on with their former noises, and add a scraping of their feet on the floor; 'a hurricane', all the former noises, and a great stamping of their feet on the floor, to make as much noise as they can.

A Hand-Book for the Teachers of Infant Schools,
Manchester and London: 1869.

A
NOVEMBER
CHILD IN
FICTION

'WON'T they hurt 'em?' asked Nat, who lay laughing with all his might.

'Oh dear, no! we always allow one pillow-fight on Saturday night. The cases are changed tomorrow; and it gets up a glow after the boys' baths; so I rather like it myself,' said Mrs Bhaer, busy again among her dozen pairs of socks.

'What a very nice school this is?' observed Nat, in a burst of admiration.

'It's an odd one,' laughed Mrs Bhaer; 'but you see we don't believe in making children miserable by too many rules, and too much study. I forbade night-gown parties at first; but, bless you, it was of no use. I could no more keep those boys in their beds, than so many jacks in the box. So I made an agreement with them: I was to allow a fifteen-minute pillow-fight every Saturday night; and they promised to go properly to bed every other night. I tried it, and it worked well. If they don't keep their word, no frolic; if they do, I just turn the glasses round, put the lamps in safe places, and let them rampage as much as they like.'

'It's a beautiful plan!' said Nat, feeling that he should like to join in the fray, but not venturing to propose it the first night. So he lay enjoying the spectacle, which certainly was a lively one.

Tommy Bangs led the assailing party, and Demi defended his own room with a dogged courage, fine to see, collecting pillows behind him as fast as they were thrown, till the besiegers were out of ammunition, when they would charge upon him in a body, and recover their arms. A few slight accidents occurred, but nobody minded, and gave and took sounding thwacks with perfect good-humour, while pillows flew like big snowflakes, till Mrs Bhaer looked at her watch, and called out –

'Time is up, boys. Into bed every man Jack, or pay the forfeit!'

'What is the forfeit?' asked Nat, sitting up in his eagerness to know what happened to those wretches who disobeyed this most peculiar, but public-spirited school-ma'am.

'Lose their fun next time,' answered Mrs Bhaer. 'I give them five minutes to settle down, then put out the lights, and expect order.

They are honourable lads, and they keep their word.'

That was evident, for the battle ended as abruptly as it began – a parting shot or two, a final cheer, as Demi fired the seventh pillow at the retiring foe, a few challenges for next time, then order prevailed; and nothing but an occasional giggle, or a suppressed whisper, broke the quiet which followed the Saturday-night frolic, as Mother Bhaer kissed her new boy, and left him to happy dreams of life at Plumfield.

Louisa May Alcott, *Little Men*, 1871.

LETTERS
from
ROYAL
NOVEMBER
CHILDREN

MARY, Princess of Orange, was born in November 1631. She addressed this letter to 'my dear lady Lillies Drummond'.

DEARE LADY LILLIES,

Beliue me I have not forgott you for nott writing to you. I loue you as well as euer I did and Prays you to continue your letters: for neuse, I pray do not expete eny from me, for I hiere non butt what comes from you, the Queene, and the Princes of Orange, and I hes had a Presant from the East Endy house; soe Pray Belieue I am constantly,

dear lady Lillies,

Your most feathfull and louing freand

MARIE.

Haye this 8 of December 1642. For my dear lady Lillies Drummond.

Letter of Charles Duke of York, written when a child to his mother Anne of Denmark (Charles I, born November, 1600):

'Most worthy mistress,

Seeing I cannot have the happiness to see your majesty, give me leave to declare by these lines the duty and love I owe to you, which makes me long to see you. I wish from my heart that I might help to find a remedy to your disease; the which I must bear the more patiently, because it is the sign of a long life. But I must for many causes be sorry; and specially because it is troublesome to you, and has deprived me of your most comfortable sight, and of many good dinners; the which I hope, by God's grace, shortly to enjoy. And when it shall please you to give me leave to see you, it may be I shall give you some good recipe, which either shall heal you or make you laugh; the which wishing I may obtain by your majesty's most gracious favour, kissing in all humility your most sacred hands, and praying for your health and long prosperity, I end, most worthy mistress,

Your majesty's most humble
and obedient servant,
CHARLES.'

RHYMES
for the
NOVEMBER
BABY

D ULL November brings the blast –
Hark! the leaves are whirling fast.

Sara Coleridge (1802–1852).

Monday's bairn is fair of face;
Tuesday's bairn is full of grace;
Wednesday's bairn's a child of woe;
Thursday's bairn has far to go;
Friday's bairn is loving and giving;
Saturday's bairn works hard for a living;

But the bairn that is born on the Sabbath-day,
Is lively and bonnie, and wise and gay.

Notes and Queries, 1862.

One old Oxford ox opening oysters;
Two tee totums totally tired of trying to
    trot to Tadberry;
Three tall tigers tippling tenpenny tea;
Four fat friars fanning fainting flies;
Five frippy Frenchmen foolishly fishing for
    flies;
Six sportsmen shooting snipes!
Seven Severn salmons swallowing shrimps;
Eight Englishmen eagerly examining Europe;
Nine nimble noblemen nibbling nonpareils;
Ten tinkers tinkling upon ten tin tinder-
    boxes with ten tenpenny tacks;
Eleven elephants elegantly equipt;
Twelve typographical topographers typi-
    cally translating types.

Nursery Rhymes of England,
collected by Halliwell, 1843.

The world is so full of a number of things,
I'm sure we should all be as happy as kings.

Robert Louis Stevenson (1850–1894).

A POEM

Still sits the school-house by the road,
  A ragged beggar sleeping;
Around it still the sumachs grow,
  And blackberry-vines are creeping.

Within, the master's desk is seen,
  Deep scarred by raps official;
The warping floor, the battered seats,
  The jack-knife's carved initial;

The charcoal frescos on its wall;
   Its door's worn sill, betraying
The feet that, creeping slow to school,
   Went storming out to playing!

Long years ago a winter sun
   Shone over it at setting;
Lit up its western window-panes,
   And low eaves' icy fretting.

It touched the tangled golden curls,
   And brown eyes full of grieving,
Of one who still her steps delayed
   When all the school were leaving.

For near her stood the little boy
   Her childish favor singled:
His cap pulled low upon a face
   Where pride and shame were mingled.

Pushing with restless feet the snow
   To right and left, he lingered; –
As restlessly her tiny hands
   The blue-checked apron fingered.

He saw her lift her eyes; he felt
　　The soft hand's light caressing,
And heard the tremble of her voice,
　　As if a fault confessing.

'I'm sorry that I spelt the word:
　　I hate to go above you,
Because,' – the brown eyes lower fell, –
　　'Because, you see, I love you!'
　　　　John Greenleaf Whittier (1807–1892).

A LULLABY

Hush-a-bye a ba-lamb,
Hush-a-bye a milk-cow;
You shall have a little stick
To beat the naughty bow-wow.
　　　　Nursery Rhymes, Tales and Jingles,
　　　　　　London, 1844.

A PRAIER TO BE SAIDE WHEN
THOU GOEST TO BEDDE

O Merciful god!
   heare this our requeste,
And graunte vnto vs
   this nighte quiet reste.
Into thy tuicion,
   oh lorde, do vs take!
Our bodies slepynge,
   our myndes yet maie wake.
Forgeue the offences
   this daye we haue wrought
Against thee and our neighbour
   in worde, dede, and thoughte!
     The School of Vertue,
      Anno. 1557.

GOODNIGHT
to the
NOVEMBER
BABY

IF amongst the presents you have been given there was a magic lamp which, if rubbed, would produce a genie who could grant your wishes, what would you ask for the new baby? Good health, of course, but would you add the usual wealth and happiness? If the short list of the distinguished born in November is anything to go by, most November babies have worked hard for their livings, so it might frustrate a great career if your baby was overloaded with genie gold. Happiness should be a perfect gift for any baby, but wishes have a way of going bad on you. Suppose your baby is to be a creative artist of some sort, the type of happiness the genie might think up could be frustrating. Anyway would you have a wish if you could?

The pattern of all our lives is so delicately woven, a strange strand in warp or woof might snarl up the whole design. You would like a blessing perhaps? Surely that could not go wrong. So bless you and your November baby. Sleep well. Goodnight.

Noel Streatfeild